GW00360327

A B D b e

F G h I J

K L M n O

Calligraphy

for Beginners

TRUDIE DEMOED

Bloomsbury Books
London

First published by Bloomsbury Books
an imprint of Godfrey Cave Associates
42 Bloomsbury Street
London WC1B 3QJ

© Godfrey Cave Associates (this edition and
presentation of material), 1994
© Savitri Books Ltd (original translation from the Dutch,
additional text and illustrations), 1994

ISBN I-85471-278-0

Conceived and designed by Savitri Books Ltd
115J Cleveland Street
London W1P 5PN

This edition is broadly based on a book by Trudie Demoed, first
published in the Netherlands in 1988 by La Riviere & Vorhoeve,
Kampen

Translation from the Dutch by Sarah Lawson
Edited by Caroline Taggart
Typeset by Dorchester Typesetting Group Ltd
Printed & bound in Great Britain

CONTENTS

INTRODUCTION

There is a huge range of books available on the subject of calligraphy. Many of them assume that the reader already has some knowledge of the subject and, consequently, gloss over or omit altogether the basic, step-by-step instructions a beginner needs to get off to a correct start. It is easy at this stage to acquire bad habits which are then difficult to lose. For a beginner, every step is important and the teacher or author must assume that the pupil knows nothing until the opposite is proved. This book therefore gives detailed instructions on such fundamental points as how the broad-nib pen should be handled; step-by-step explanations show how individual letters are put together, strung into words and sentences, then finally presented to form a well-balanced page.

This book encourages the student to copy the examples given until the rules are mastered and confidence grows. The aim is eventually to develop a personal style by applying the knowledge gained. This principle can then be extended to other kinds of script.

If you are left-handed, you may think that calligraphy is not for you. Do not be deterred: special oblique-handled nibs will make your task easier. This book also contains instructions specific to left-handers. These are not iron rules but guidelines designed to help you. With a little trial and error you will soon discover what works for you.

SCRIPTS & THEIR ORIGINS

The three and a half centuries which followed the fall of the Roman Empire until the rise of Charlemagne were a turbulent period. In all areas of life, the once unified Roman order was breaking down and this affected writing, along with everything else. The uncial script used by scribes towards the end of the Roman Empire gradually developed into half-uncial script – the origin of the modern minuscules (lower case or 'small' letters). In a continent where the sophisticated communication systems which had developed during the Roman era were drastically breaking down, it is not surprising that different styles of writing evolved in the various parts of the former empire. The most important of these variations were: the Irish and Anglo-Saxon script in Ireland and Britain, the Merovingian and East Frankish script in France and Germany, Longobardic script in Northern Italy, the script of Montecasino and Benevente in Southern Italy, Papal Curial script and the West Gothic or Visigothic script in Spain. Examples of some of these early scripts are shown opposite. They provide a fascinating insight into the development of handwriting and also of type.

All these scripts are nowadays lumped together under the name of Pre-Carolingian scripts. Although they varied enormously, they had one important feature in common: they all, to a greater or lesser extent, adopted word division within each line. The use of majuscules (capitals) and minuscules, which had previously been mixed more or less at random, was regulated for the first time. This had not been the norm in Roman times, and the development greatly improved legibility. Under the influence of Charlemagne, who was trying to unify his empire, a new style evolved which became known as Carolingian script (from Carolus, the Latin for Charles). In 789 the Emperor ordered that all existing texts – both religious and

Anglo-Saxon script

Carolingian minuscules from the
scribes' school of Tours

Merovingian script

Carolingian minuscules
(10th century)

Pre-Carolingian script
(AD 800)

Carolingian minuscules
(12th century)

secular – be copied in Carolingian script, and this became the official writing style throughout the empire, which covered most of northern Europe.

This script presents many features which can be found in present-day writing, especially in the clear word and line divisions and in the use of serifs. It used a fairly constant nib position of 30 degrees and an x-height of about four-nib widths. It is based on the round 'O' shape.

Between the tenth and the twelfth centuries this round form developed into an oval which finally broke up to produce the typical Gothic form.

GOTHIC SCRIPT

The broken shape of the typical Gothic letter is seen by some authorities as an interruption in the progress of the Carolingian minuscule. Others see the introduction of Gothic letters as forming part of a continuous line – an evolution which finally resulted in the Humanistic minuscule on the one hand and the Humanistic cursive, or italic, on the other hand. Part of a Gothic alphabet, upper and lower case, is shown opposite.

When we study the separate letter shapes and look how each one is made up, we see that the Carolingian minuscule was written with connecting upstrokes and that the script was slightly slanted to the right. These characteristics ensured that the script could be written at considerable speed.

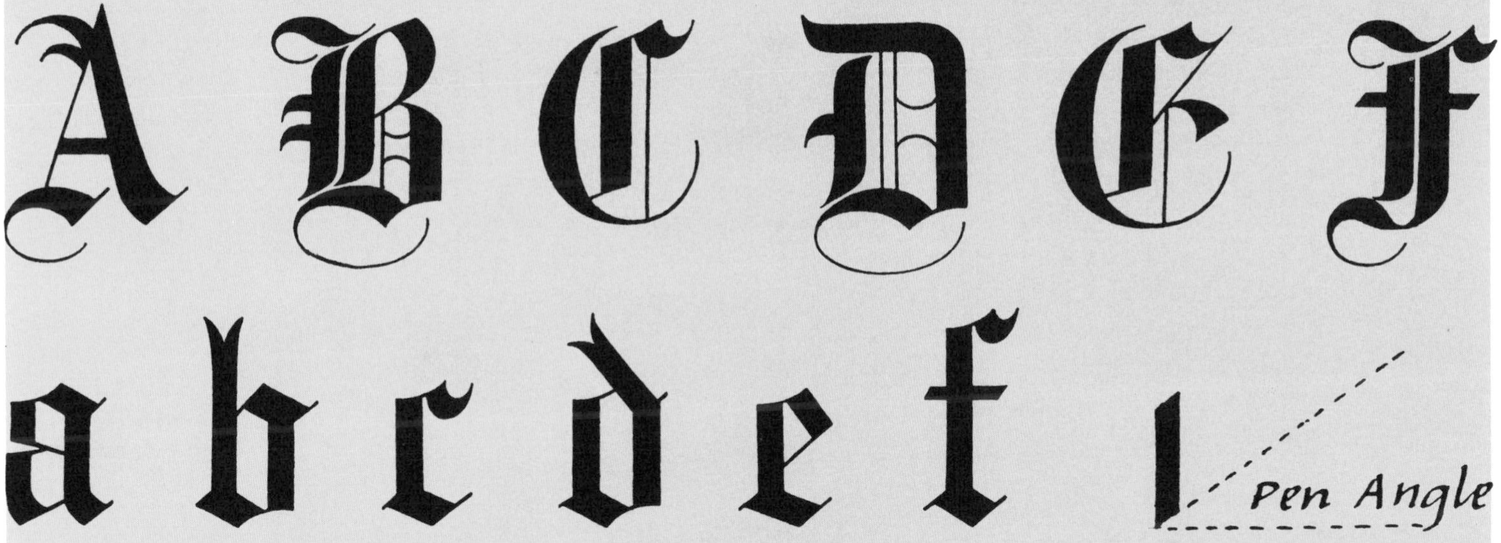

A B C D E F

a b c d e f

Pen Angle

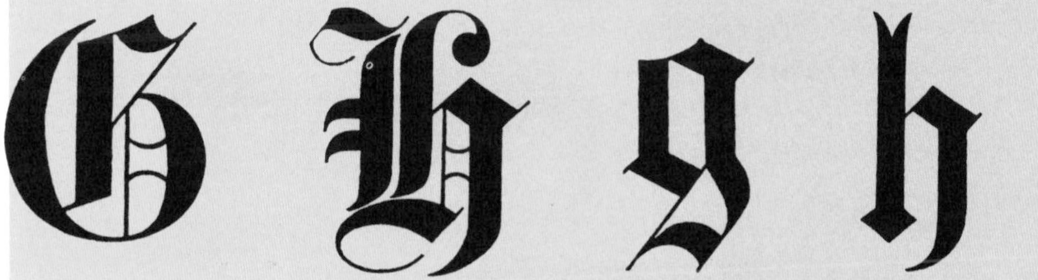

G H g h

A black letter or Gothic alphabet. Note that the white space inside each letter is about equal to the area of black in the letter form. In the alphabet shown here, the pen angle is about 35 degrees for most strokes, but the angle is changed a little for parts of 'A', 'G', 'S' and 'Z', as you will notice if you look closely.

Two Gothic forms of writing evolved from this Carolingian minuscule. In one the letters were still executed with connected upstrokes, although these were not visible as such. The styles known as Fraktur and Bastarda, illustrated on page 15, are examples of this.

The other form evolved as a script with angular flourishes or curves and descenders such as Textura and Rotunda, illustrated opposite. These scripts are considerably more 'static' in appearance, they cannot be written so quickly and they are more suitable for a formal book hand than for everyday handwriting.

The main spheres of influence under which the various kinds of scripts flowered were those ruled by the Emperor on the one hand and the Pope on the other. The Alps formed a natural dividing line between the two.

HUMANISTIC SCRIPT

During the Renaissance there was a new interest in the ancient world. Art and science revived after the dark period of the Middle Ages. However, the sixteenth-century scholars frequently referred to copies of old documents that Charlemagne had had transcribed into Carolingian script. People were impressed by these letter forms and mistook them for an older classical script of the ancient world. At first, they called the script 'Littera Antiqua' – old letter' – and developed a style of writing based on it.

If we look at the construction of the Carolingian minuscule, Textura, Rotunda and

mo
Carolingian minuscules

mo
Fraktur

mo
Bastarda

mo
Textura

mo
Rotunda

mo
Humanistic minuscules

Humanistic minuscule in that order, a certain pattern of the evolution is clear. It is also obvious that the form of the Humanistic minuscule is directly copied from the Carolingian minuscule and influenced by both Textura and Rotunda.

The texture of the Humanistic minuscule, which consists of downstrokes and curves, is an ideal starting point for the beginner to learn to understand the alphabetic forms and their connection with each other. The interplay of construction and appearance makes the Humanistic minuscule the prototype of our modern printed letter in its Roman form.

FOUNDATIONAL ROUND HAND

In the period following the Renaissance handwriting fell under the influence of engraving and it became fashionable for the first time to write with a pointed nib. In the course of a few centuries the use of the broad nib fell into oblivion, and it was not until the beginning of the twentieth century that Edward Johnston rediscovered this instrument. With the tenth-

Left. Copperplate, written
with a pointed nib.

Below. Based on the tenth-century
Winchester Psalter.

mo.

Et hacc scribimus
vobis ut gaudeatis,
& gaudium vestrum
sit plenum.

Et hacc est annunciatio, quam
audivimus ab eo, & annunciamus
vobis : Quoniam Deus lux est.
& tenebrae in eo non sunt ullae..

century Winchester Psalter *as a point of departure, he developed a modern script for students of calligraphy with the round 'o' form as its basis: he called it the Foundational Round Hand. The scripts taught in this book are strongly influenced by this development.*

Garamond GARAMOND!
PLANTIN—?
Palatino Q &
Bembo ∾ Times

Many modern typefaces such as Bembo, Baskerville, Times, Plantin, Garamond and others are based on the Humanistic script.

P Q R S T

U V X Y Z

These handsome capitals belong to a widely used style of lettering which appeared throughout Europe in the thirteenth century. The first part of this alphabet appears opposite the title page of this book.

EQUIPMENT

One of the joys of calligraphy is that it is easy to start with a minimum of equipment and space. All you really need is a drawing board, a chair, paper, pens and ink.

A drawing board of some sort is essential. These can often be bought second-hand or you can make one yourself by using an old pastry board, or a piece of stout plywood or formica – indeed anything with a smooth surface and measuring at least 50 × 70 cm (20 × 28 in). This can then sit on a steady table at an appropriate height. The board should be angled at approximately 30 degrees (a little less for left-handers). This helps the flow of the ink: if you work on a flat surface, your pen may 'flood'. The bottom of the board should be about 20 cm (8 in) above your lap. If you use a plain wooden board, place a block of wood of appropriate thickness under its end to achieve the required slope.

Alternatively, you can make your own adjustable drawing board to fit on a table, at little cost and effort. The sketch on page 20 will show you how it is constructed.

It is also very important to sit at the right height in relation to the board, with your feet resting comfortably on the ground. Trying to work in a cramped position will result in painful cramps and sloppy work. A swivel chair with adjustable height is the best option and if you are going to spend a lot of time writing, it is an investment well worth considering.

Good light is vital. It should come from the left if you are right-handed and from the right for a left-handed person.

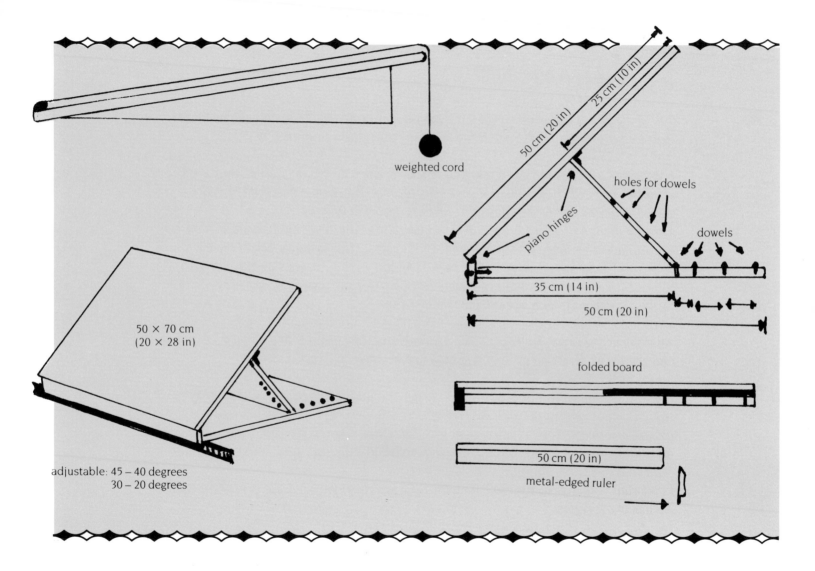

weighted cord

50 cm (20 in)

25 cm (10 in)

holes for dowels

piano hinges

dowels

35 cm (14 in)

50 cm (20 in)

50 × 70 cm
(20 × 28 in)

folded board

50 cm (20 in)

metal-edged ruler

adjustable: 45 – 40 degrees
30 – 20 degrees

PAPER

For the purposes of practice any smooth-surfaced paper is fine. Lay-out paper, for instance, would be excellent. It comes in pads in sizes ranging from A1 to A5. But 80 or 120 gsm photocopying paper or ordinary white drawing paper also makes an excellent exercise paper. For final work, you must use a hot-pressed or hand-made paper. Use the smooth side. Very often this sort of paper bears a watermark which will then read the right way round.

THE WRITING SURFACE

If you use a simple writing board with a block under the top end to make it slope, line it with card, blotting paper or even several layers of newspaper. The sheet on which you are going to work can then be held in position with strong elastic bands or weighted cords (see a) opposite). This method was used in a typical scriptorium in the Middle Ages.

If you are using a proper drawing board – see b) opposite – it must be lined in the same manner. Pin a piece of strong paper with its upper part just below what you regard as the most comfortable writing position (see illustration on the right). The top section of the writing paper is held in place with a tape going right

guard sheet

round the board. The position of the writing paper can be easily adjusted by pulling it up as more lines are worked. The guard sheet protects your work from accidental spillage.

MATERIALS & INSTRUMENTS

You will need pencils for ruling up paper; and they are also useful for beginners' exercises. Pencils are sold in various degrees of hardness: 9H is the hardest, then 8, 7, 6, 5, 4, 3, 2H and H. HB is of medium hardness. Softer grades are B, 2, 3, 4, 5, 6, 7, 8 and 9B.
Buy a ruler at least 50 cm (20 in) long with a metal strip along one edge. This kind of ruler is handy if you are drawing lines with ink or paint, using a drawing pen. A rather soft rubber — not plastic — eraser, and a pencil sharpener or pocket knife are also necessary.

You can use ink of any kind; watercolour diluted to the consistency of ink; gouache or poster paint. Fountain-pen ink is excellent to practise with. Black Indian ink is the best medium for final work as it dries to a solid black, and is light and waterproof. Remember that the pen nib will have to be cleaned frequently as Indian ink dries quickly and would clog it up. Nibs must also be cleaned thoroughly after use and dried carefully or they will rust. Avoid coloured inks for final work, as they will fade quickly in the light. For colour work, use watercolour or gouache.

The most important piece of equipment is a selection of nibs and pen-holders. These may look a long way from the reed pens used some 3000 years ago, yet they and goose or swan quills used by medieval scribes were cut to an edge and it was the discovery of this shape in the nineteenth century which led to the development of the modern chisel nib used by most Western calligraphers today.

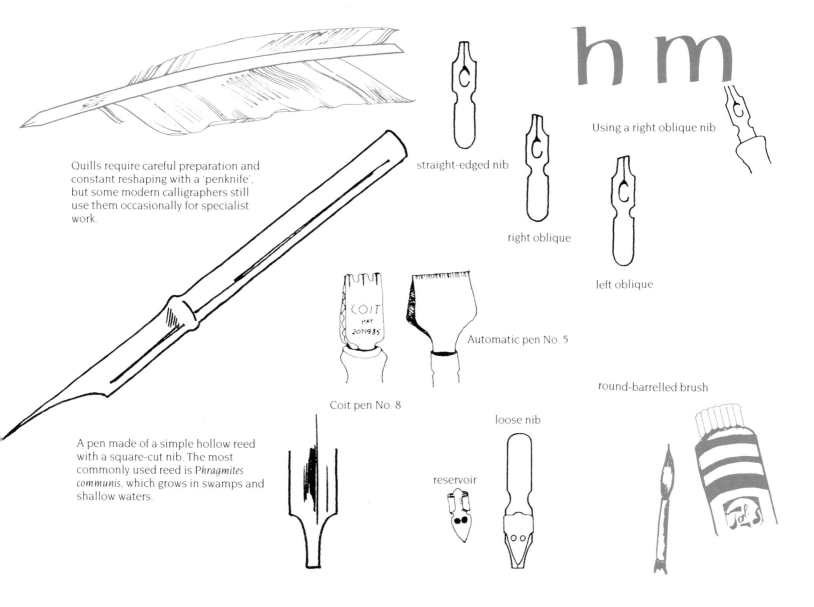

Quills require careful preparation and constant reshaping with a 'penknife', but some modern calligraphers still use them occasionally for specialist work.

straight-edged nib

right oblique

left oblique

Using a right oblique nib

h m

A pen made of a simple hollow reed with a square-cut nib. The most commonly used reed is *Phragmites communis*, which grows in swamps and shallow waters.

Coit pen No. 8

COIT
PAT
2071985

Automatic pen No. 5

reservoir

loose nib

round-barrelled brush

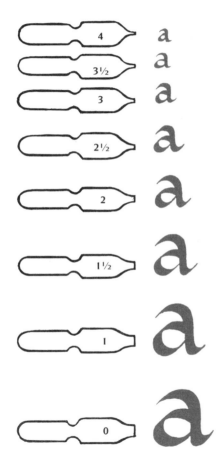

Nibs come in a variety of sizes, starting with size 6 which is the smallest, to size 00 which is the largest. You are unlikely to use size 5 or 6, as they produce such small letters. Opposite you will see the letter sizes produced by a range of nibs.

Nibs can be oblique – left or right – or straight cut (see illustration on previous page). Most people will use the straight one but a left-oblique nib is useful for left-handed people and for Arabic or Hebrew calligraphy, which is written right to left.

You can use an ordinary pen-holder with your nibs, but you will need to buy a detachable reservoir, as shown on page 23. The reservoir is filled with a brush, using ink or watercolour diluted to the appropriate consistency. It ensures that the ink flows evenly as you write. You can also buy a special pen-holder with a built-in reservoir (see below). The reservoir here consists of a tiny metal strip which stores the ink. If you use thinned watercolour, try to mix a quantity sufficient to complete the work or a self-contained part of it – you may not obtain exactly the same colour again. Store the liquid in a small pot with an airtight lid. If you want to produce really large letters, witch pens are useful. They start with size 1 and the largest is size 4.

The most commonly used sizes of nibs and the letter sizes they produce.

pen-holder with built-in reservoir

MAKING YOUR FIRST MARK

for right-handers

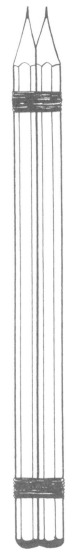

You will need:
A few sheets of drawing paper
2 HB pencils
Tape, eraser, pencil sharpener
Automatic pen No. 5 or Coit pen No. 8 (see page 23)
Tube of poster paint, saucer and jam jar
Round brush
Jar with lid
Rag or paper towels
Triangle, with angles of 30, 60 and 90 degrees,
the longest side not exceeding 20 cm (8 in)

You will start this exercise with the pencils, keeping the pen for later when you have acquired a little confidence. Hold both pencils together and do some practice writing. This is to get your hand used to the thickness of the pencils.

Sharpen your two pencils to a fine point. Fasten them together at the upper end and just above the points, using rubber bands or sellotape as shown. If you are right-handed, you can keep the points even, as shown on the right, or somewhat slanted in relation to each other, with the right point slightly higher than the left (like the straight and right-oblique nibs).

for left-handers

You will soon discover how much of a slant you need by working with the two pencils. When you work, you should exert an equal amount of pressure on both points to produce two parallel lines of equal thickness. Hold the double pencil with a relaxed grip.

The basic principle of calligraphy is the pen position. A square-cut nib and/or a double pencil automatically produce varying thick or thin lines depending upon the angle at which they are held. Indeed, every nib angle gives the letter a different shape, as can be seen in the examples of the letter 'g' below. The nib is being held at an angle of 45 degrees with the baseline.

The nib angle means the angle that the nib makes with the baseline in order to draw the thinnest possible line. It is nothing to do with the angle at which you hold your pen. Different styles of writing therefore call for different nib angles. Being able to determine and to maintain the same nib angle within a piece worked in a particular hand, is the underlying principle of good calligraphy.

The alphabet we are primarily studying in this book has a nib angle of 30 degrees. That means that the thinnest possible line makes an angle of 30 degrees with the baseline.

By way of illustration, let us visualise a drawing of a clock. The circular face divides into 360 degrees – four blocks of 90. The hours divide the circle into twelve parts which fall every 30 degrees (12 × 30 = 360). On your practice sheet, draw a circle with the baseline as diameter and divide this into twelve sections. The baseline/diameter runs from 9 o'clock to 3 o'clock and has no angle. If we now move both ends of the baseline/diameter by one hour, we move 30 degrees. If we draw a line from 8 o'clock to 2 o'clock, this makes an angle of 30 degrees to the diameter/baseline.

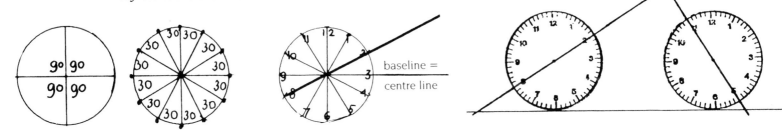

The pen position is dictated by the thinnest possible line; both the points of the double pencil must therefore be in a position of 8 o'clock to 2 o'clock to make the pencil (or pen's) position 30 degrees. The thickest possible line is always perpendicular to the thinnest possible line (see drawings).

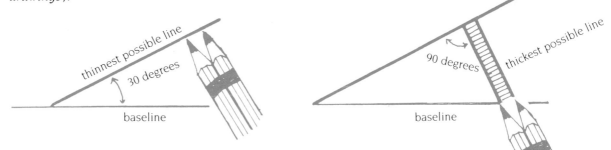

Of course, you don't have to keep drawing the clock, but bear it in mind: use the line from 11 o'clock to 5 o'clock when you practise the 30 degree nib angle. You can use the circle again to work out the 45 degree angle which is used for other styles of writing, such as the Round Hand alphabet. Do the exercises which follow first, using the double-pencil method. When you feel confident that you can do these exercises evenly and can maintain the angle of your thin and thick lines accurately, it is time to start practising with a pen nib.

FITTING THE NIB

Set the nib into the pen-holder so that its tip is about 3 mm (⅛ in) from the tip of the reservoir, which should just touch the nib. If the latter exerts undue pressure, the slit in the nib will open up – hold it up to the light to check – and you will have to adjust the reservoir. Similarly, if contact is not made, remove the nib or the reservoir, if detachable, and slip it on again, ensuring that it now touches the nib.

INKING THE NIB

The reservoir should now be filled using the brush. Be careful not to overfill the reservoir or the pen may 'flood'. Always keep the ink bottle on the same side as your writing hand, never stretch over the work to refill your pen. When working on a final piece, it is good practice to try out a nib every time you fill it, on a piece of paper which you keep pinned to the upper right-hand (left if you are left-handed) corner of the board, to make sure the ink flows well.

PEN TO PAPER

The whole of the flat end of the nib must touch the paper and you should exert just enough pressure to enable the ink to flow evenly. The slit in the pen should not open. Your left hand (your right, if you are left-handed) should rest on the guard sheet, close to your writing hand. The sketches below show the hand position for right-handed and left-handed writing.

holding the pen
a) left-handers
b) right-handers

Using an HB pencil draw yourself guidelines as shown in the exercise below. Remember the points about maintaining the correct angles throughout the piece of work. If the pen is held at the correct angle, the upstroke will produce the hairline – the finest possible line which can be produced by a particular nib – while the downstroke makes the broadest possible line. Later on when you come to practise with letters, you can always check that you are holding your pen at the correct angle by working a sample of this simple pattern. The nib is held at a 45 degree angle.

Now try the pattern below. Note that the thin and the thick strokes are at exactly the same angle as before. These two exercises are a preliminary to forming letters.

innocent

Pay extra attention to the hairlines. They form a vital part of many calligraphic styles. They should never become thick. You will notice that where there is no hairline as between the letters 'o' and 'c', an equivalent space has been left.

TROUBLE-SHOOTING

It is now time to look back at your work and see if you have been experiencing difficulties using the pen. There are several reasons why the ink may not flow satisfactorily:

a)   The tip of the nib may not be in full contact with the paper.

b)   You may not have relaxed your hand while writing or you may be holding the pen in an exaggeratedly vertical position or too close to the paper surface.

c)   The ink may be too tacky – try another make. If you are writing on hot-pressed paper, the surface may be too smooth or slightly greasy, and this prevents the ink from flowing freely. Try rubbing the paper surface with a small amount of scouring powder and a soft cloth. Remove every trace of the powder before continuing with your work. You could also try adding a minute amount of a liquid detergent to the ink or paint to help with the flow.

d)   The nib may require cleaning, or it may be old or defective, causing the slit to open.

Here are some further examples of patterns for you to practise on. Make sure you keep your work even and neat and that the up and downstrokes always rest on the guidelines. The small diamonds are a tiny part of a downstroke and will be useful for punctuation and dots over the letters 'i' and 'j'. These patterns will also come in useful later on when you work on a text and need a design to fill out the end of a line.

31

The other basic shape of the alphabet is the curve. We distinguish between the curve with the opening to the right and the curve with the opening to the left.

The curve with the opening to the right: after drawing the guidelines start from the top and make a half-circle, which should touch the bottom line in one spot only. The interior space should form a perfect semicircle.

The curve with the opening to the left: this is a mirror image of the previous curve. Start from the top again. Complete the circle without going over the hairline of the other curve, which would become thick. The inner space should now be a perfect circle.

The exercises shown opposite were done using a broad-nib pen, either a Coit No. 8 or an Automatic Pen No. 5, and poster paint. Before opening a tube of poster paint for the first time, you must 'massage' the paint. Sometimes the gum that keeps the paint flexible collects at the top of the tube. Kneading the closed tube mixes the gum with the paint again. When you open the tube discard any excess gum. Always clean the top of the tube before shutting it.

Put some poster paint in a little pot, pressing not more than ½ cm (¼ in) out of the tube. Then add about 5 cc (2 fl oz) water drop by drop with a pipette. Mix the water and paint with a paintbrush. The mixture should not be too watery or transparent, but sufficiently liquid to flow properly when you are writing.

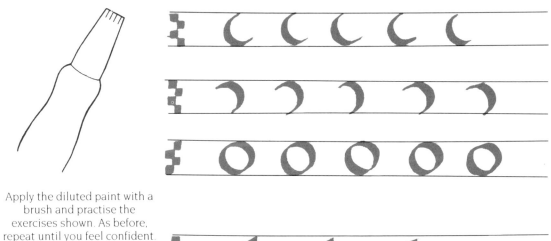

Apply the diluted paint with a
brush and practise the
exercises shown. As before,
repeat until you feel confident.

You will now have mastered all the basic strokes and forming minuscules — lower case letters —
will be much simpler. We'll start with the Humanistic hand in which the nib is held at a 30
degree angle. All these preambles and exercises might seem to have gone on for ever but
you'll reap the benefits of this careful preparation when you embark on your first piece of
'proper' work.

GLORIA in excelsis Deo

et in terra PAX

THE ALPHABET AS A FAMILY

If we look at the 26 letters of the alphabet, the minuscules or lower-case letters obviously form a family of which the letters 'i' and 'o' are the basic forms.

The other 24 letters are descended from these two, yet every letter has, besides features of the 'o' or the 'i', its own identity which must be evident whatever style of writing is chosen.

The letter 'i'. The sketch shows how it is made. Note that the dot over 'i' and 'j' can be produced in two ways. The first is by making a little stroke over the full width of the letter and serif. The starting point lies on the top line, exactly above the beginning of the serif, and goes in the same direction as the whole letter. The other way is to form a dot in the shape of a comma. The starting point is exactly above the downstroke. The comma is drawn at an angle of 30 degrees to the left, ending thin on the top line.

On the page opposite appears the entire Humanistic alphabet. Over the next few pages you will find detailed instructions on how to form the individual letters. The majuscules or capitals appear on page 53.

The letter 'y' can be done in 3 different ways, as shown in the alphabet opposite.

a b c d e f g

h i j k l m n

o p q r s t u

v w x y y y z

The letter 'o'. The nib is placed on the top line at a 30 degree angle. The curve with the opening to the right is drawn. The inside space should be a perfect semicircle. The nib is positioned one nib-width from the top in the just finished curve. The opposite curve is drawn until it touches the right-hand curve. The finished 'o' should be not round but oval, the two curves overlapping slightly at the 'seams'.

The letter 'a'. It starts out like 'o', as shown, but the line then goes straight down and ends with a small curve, like that of the letter 'i'. Directly under the beginning of the right half curve, start with the lowest part of the left curve of the 'o'. Finally, the first and second strokes are connected by a thin line.

The letter 'b'. The total height of the 'b' is seven times the nib-width. The ascender rises three times the nib-width above the height of a small letter (the x-height). This also applies to the ascenders of the letters d, h, k and l. Measure the distance of three times the nib-width above the top line and draw a horizontal line. Against this line make the first part of the serif and then a perpendicular downstroke. When you approach the baseline, put in the lowest part of the left-hand curve of the 'o'. Put the nib on the downstroke and make the right-hand arc of the 'o'. Finish off the serif.

The letter 'c'. Draw the left-hand arc of the 'o'. Place the nib on the starting point of this shape and draw the upper side of the 'c' rather flat along the top line. This is not an 'o' with a section missing – the 'c' is more open.

The letter 'd'. First make a 'c' as described above. At a point three times the nib-width above the top line begin the serif and draw the downstroke towards the base line. End the downstroke in a little curve like that of the 'i'. Finish off the serif. The 'c' and the downstroke overlap by one nib width.

The letter 'e'. Draw the left-hand arc of the 'o'. Place the pen point on the starting point of this form and make the loop. This must end just above the mid-point of the letter (or the left-hand arc of the 'o').

The letter 'f'. This is the longest letter of the alphabet. From the top to the baseline, the letter is seven times the nib-width. Below the baseline the descender is an extra three times the width of the nib. Three nib-widths above the top line, begin the rounded stroke and draw it straight downwards after a slight bend. The perpendicular stroke ends three times the nib-width below the baseline and bends to the left. Place the nib at the beginning of the first stroke and draw the top side of the 'c'. Just at the top draw the crossbar. This has a firm horizontal form and ends straight below the interior space of the second stroke. The crossbar should not go over the top line.

The letter 'g'. First make a 'c'. Place the nib a half-width to the right of the 'c' on the top line. Draw the downstroke with a slight bend into the 'c' and straight on down to three times the nib-width below the baseline. The letter ends there with a slight bend to the left, like the 'f'. The tail of the 'g' is made like the second stroke of the 'a' and is located exactly under the 'c' form. The length of the tail is a maximum of four nib-widths below the baseline.

The letter 'h'. At a point three times the nib-width above the top line make the beginning of the serif and then make the downstroke perpendicular towards the baseline. The stroke is closed off with a tiny rounded ending. Place the nib point in the downstroke and make the first stroke of the letter 'a'. Finish off the serif.

41

The letter 'j'. Make the beginning of the serif and then the perpendicular downstroke like that of the 'f'. Finish off the serif. Dot the 'j' as described on page 35. If you prefer, the downstroke can be made like the descender of the 'g' (see previous page).

The letter 'k'. Make the long down-stroke like that of the 'h'. Place the nib one nib-width from the downstroke on the top line (30 degrees), place the nib on the downstroke and then make the curve and the diagonal. Finish off the serif.

The letter 'l'. Make the long downstroke of the 'b', with the broad, rounded stroke. Finish off the serif.

The letter 'm'. Make the downstroke of the 'i' with the small, rounded stroke of the 'h' and 'k' at the bottom. Finish off the serif, but do not take the pen off the paper as you reach the downstroke. Directly from the downstroke, make the first stroke of the letter 'a', again with a little, rounded stroke. Place the nib in the second downstroke and make the same stroke once again, now with the rounded stroke of the 'i' on the baseline.

You can also make the 'm' in the following manner:

The letter 'n'. Make the downstroke like that of the 'm'. Finish off the serif, joining to it the first stroke of the letter 'a'.

You can also make the 'n' as shown overleaf:

The letter 'p'. Make the downstroke like that of the 'j'. Finish off the serif and proceed immediately with the right-hand arc of the 'o'. Place the nib in the downstroke and draw a somewhat flattened round form to the right-hand arc of the 'o'. The round bit of the 'p' is the 'c' form in reverse.

You can also make the 'p' as follows:

The letter 'q'. Make the letter 'c' as described on page 39. Draw the downstroke like that of the 'g', but end it in a straight line. A short, straight serif is placed to the right of the straight downstroke to make a clear distinction between 'g' and 'q'.

The letter 'r'. Make the 'i' form. Finish the serif and draw the rounded stroke to the place where this blends into the downstroke.

The 'r' can also be worked as follows:

The letter 's'. This is a difficult one. To prevent it from falling backwards or forwards you can start by tracing a little box for it to fit into before beginning to write. Here, too, there are two ways of tracing the letter. In the first one you make the characteristic serpentine form, then draw the second stroke of the 'c', and finally add the third stroke of the 'p'.

The second method consists of making the second stroke of the letter 'c', then the third stroke of the 'p'. These two strokes are connected by the serpentine form.

The letter 't'. Place the nib on the top line and draw a short line in the direction of the nib upwards until you reach one nib-width above the top line. Join to that the downstroke like that of the 'l' and the 'b'. To make the crossbar, which lies on the underside of the top line, the nib is placed in the first position. The horizontal stroke to the right ends directly above the end of the first stroke.

The letter 'u'. Make the start of the serif and connect the downstroke with the curve like that of 'b', 'i' and 't'. Draw the second stroke in the shape of an 'i'. The curve of the first downstroke and the second downstroke overlap by one nib-width. Finish off the serif.

The letters 'v', 'w', 'x', 'y' and 'z' are the odd ones out. All these letters except the 'z' have a sloping downstroke to the right. This is called a diagonal. All these diagonals are written with a pen angle of 45 degrees, in order to produce a stroke of the same thickness as in the other letters.

The letter 'v'. Place the nib with a pen angle of 45 degrees half a nib-width from the top line. The first stroke begins with a small, rounded stroke on the top line and then goes diagonally to the baseline. The second, somewhat curved stroke is made with a pen angle of 30 degrees.

The letter 'w'. First make a 'v'. Beginning in the bend of the second stroke, make the other 'v' to complete the letter 'w'.

The letter 'x'. With the pen at a 45 degree angle, make the first stroke, somewhat more sloping to the right than the strokes of the 'v' and 'w'. The second stroke, with a pen angle of 30 degrees, begins with a serif drawn from left to right, just touching the top line. Draw the diagonal with a serif on the baseline going firmly to the right.

The letter 'y'. There are two methods. In the first a 'v' is made as described earlier. Draw straight down from the lowest point of the 'v' and end with a serif like that of a 'q'.

Alternatively, make the 'v', but let the second stroke continue as far as three times the nib-width below the baseline and end it as with the 'p', 'j' and 'f'.

The letter 'z'. The 'z' has no clear relation to the 'o' or 'i'. It is written in one stroke. To prevent it falling over in either direction, trace a box as you did for 's' until you can write this letter unaided.

Punctuation marks. Full stops, commas and others must be written with the same care as the letters. The full stop can be placed on the baseline or in the middle between the base and the top lines. In order to produce a clean diamond shape, position the pen at a 45 degree angle. This applies to all punctuation. The comma is placed in the same way as a full stop. Start it in the same way, but give the comma its shape by making a rounded thin stroke to the left.

Colon and semi-colon. These are placed between the baseline and the top line. Quotation marks are placed so that they just touch the top line.

Question and exclamation marks. These are again written holding the pen at a 45 degree angle. They are seven times the nib-width in height, thus shorter than letters with ascenders – 'b', 'd', 'h', 'k' and 'l'. In writing the question mark, first work the serpentine shape, then place the full stop directly under it.

For the exclamation mark, make the beginning of the serif and the downstroke. Finish the serif and place the full stop below the downstroke.

the quick brown fox jumps over the lazy dog

You have now learnt how to form all the minuscules or lower-case letters of the alphabet and can begin to write in earnest. The sentence shown above includes all the letters of the alphabet. The rules for letter spacing are the same as those outlined on page 60. The width of a lower case 'o' should be left between words.

CAPITAL LETTERS

When the Carolingian script came to be widely used, rules for the use of capitals also evolved. Generally the first lines of a piece of text were written in Roman capitals. The beginning of a paragraph was marked by uncial letters. A sentence was begun with a large, outsize minuscule. During the Renaissance the lines already looked like the ones we use today. Many different styles of capitals have evolved since then — both in writing and in printing — yet all are based on the Roman capitals.

Opposite you will find an alphabet of capitals which will ally themselves well with the lower-case letters you have been studying. The basic shape is again the round 'o'. The nib angle is still 30 degrees. The serifs are like those of the minuscules. The height of the capitals is slightly less than the height of the ascender letters — 'b', 'd', 'h', 'l' and 'k' — and is about 6½ times the nib-width. The capitals also form a family. A circle in a square is the basic drawn shape. Not all letters are the same width: there are groups of round, very narrow, narrow, wide and very wide letters. You must commit these different groups to memory.

To understand the form well, you should first draw the letters in their proper proportion with a pencil. After that, write words and characteristic sentences with a pencil to learn to estimate the spacing properly, then start with a pen. The order of the strokes is indicated by the numbered arrows.

O CGQDH

AV UTXN

YZBEFKL

PRSIJMW

NUMERALS

They are the same size as capital letters and are written between two guidelines. The pen angle is 30 degrees.

The order of the strokes is indicated by numbered arrows.

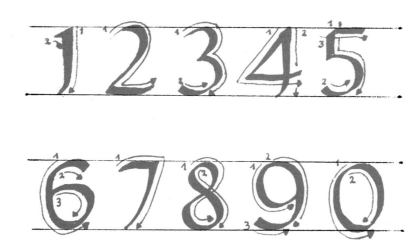

CHOOSING THE PEN SIZE

The height or size of letters is indicated by the term 'x-height'. This is the height of letters such as 'a', 'c', 'e' – indeed of all letters without ascenders or descenders. The expression comes from the printing world: only the letter 'x' has four serifs and can therefore be measured accurately.

In a Humanistic letter, the height of a lower-case 'a' should be four times the width of the nib. Therefore the pen size is determined by the height of letter you require.

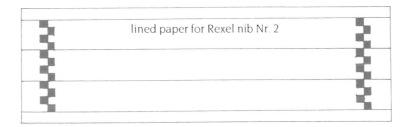

lined paper for Rexel nib Nr. 2

The space height is generally equal to or slightly greater than the text height, but this may vary greatly depending on the character and length of the text you are working on.

DRAWING GUIDELINES

Before you start writing, you must draw guidelines. It is vital to learn to do this accurately as it forms a very important part of the calligrapher's craft.

On a stout strip of paper 3 cm (1 ¼ in) wide and 10 cm (4 in) long, mark off the nib-width four times on both sides. Do this three times, one under the other. Use a different strip of paper for every nib size. (See sketch on previous page, which shows the prepared strip obtained by using a Rexel nib No. 2.)

Let's say that we use a space height equal to twice the x-height. On your lined strip of paper the distance is of one line and one line space.

Lay your sheet of A3 or A4 writing paper on a piece of blotting paper. From the top of the writing paper measure off 4 cm (1 ½ in) on both sides. Make dots, using a well-sharpened pencil. A hard pencil, 3H or 4H, works more precisely than a soft pencil, HB or H. But remember that it is harder to erase. Make sure that you work very lightly so that the marks will not leave lines or furrows in the paper when you come to erase them.

Now lay the lined strip appropriate to the nib you are going to use on the paper, first to the right, then to the left-hand side: place dots at the lines that mark the x-height and the space between the lines. Next connect the dot with a fine line. (See the sketches opposite.)

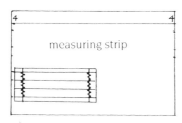

measuring strip

Marking the position
of the guidelines

The prepared sheet of
writing paper

It is a good idea to mark each text space
with a bracket — this ensures that you will
not accidentally write within the space
height. (See sketch.)

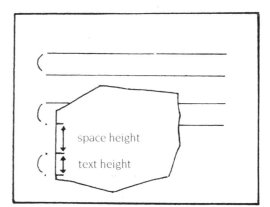

space height

text height

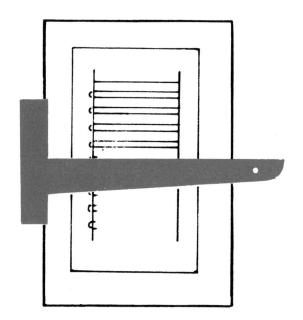

If you have a T-square it will simplify the task of ruling up and it also ensures greater accuracy than using a ruler. Fasten the piece of writing paper to the drawing board with its edges parallel to those of the board. Ensure that the 'head' of the T-square is flush with the edge of the drawing board. Using the T-square vertically first, draw two vertical lines to indicate the approximate limits within which you intend to work. Down the first line mark the text and space heights using the measurements on the paper strip you prepared earlier. Then turning the T-square to the horizontal position, draw lines exactly through the dots: accuracy is vital.

LETTER FORMS

Single letters do not tell us much by themselves. They have meaning only in combination with other letters when they form a word. The overall image of a word is what we recognize, and that recognition is one of the prerequisites for being able to read. Therefore the image of a word must be clear, and it can only be clear if the letter forms are in balance with interior and exterior space.

The exterior space is called spacing or white space. The letter form encloses the interior space. In open letters like 'a', 's', 'k', 'r', 'e' and 't', the interior and exterior spaces overflow into each other. The letter forms and the spaces that exist because of these forms are equally important. The creation of a proper play of form and space in words, sentences and texts is one of the most difficult, but at the same time most absorbing, activities of the calligrapher. Only by looking critically, and by practising with the eye and hand, can you master it.

WORD DESIGN

It is important to realize the visual impact the positioning of individual letters has within a word. This is again something which needs to be acquired through practice, but there are a few basic rules:

a) Two vertical strokes stand fairly far from each other.

b) A vertical and a round stroke stand somewhat closer together. The extra space that appears because of the round form must be as it were counterbalanced in the middle.

c) Two round strokes stand almost touching each other. This balances the space.

The examples below illustrate these basic principles. The word 'loophole' shows two round letters together. The position of the second 'l' is interesting, as is that of the 'o' between the letters with ascenders.

loophole

Do try it for yourself, practising on various words and similar combinations of letters. You should write in groups of three letters: the letter form which is already written is the point of departure for the letter that follows. In writing the second letter, you should already be thinking about the third, etc. For example, if an 'o' comes after an 'r', then that 'r' is written differently from when an 'a' comes after the 'r'. In this example the 'r' has adapted to its surroundings by joining with the starting stroke of the letter 'a'. In this way the spacing remains the same to the eye.

rora

If both 'r's were made in the same way, the space between 'r' and 'a' would appear exaggerated. To counterbalance this, the distance between the first 'r' and the 'o' has been increased. This emphasizes the need to 'think ahead'.

EXTENDING & CONDENSING LINES

A line of text can be extended by increasing the spaces between the words. But care must be taken not to produce a 'loose' line. Similarly, spaces can be narrowed to get the line to fit. Here again, this device should be used sparingly. Round letters can be crossed and ligatures introduced in 'ff', 'tt', 'th', 'rr'; the ampersand (&) can be substituted for the word 'and'. Capitals can occasionally slip within or above another capital or lower-case letter to take up less space.

ft ta ta aa en æ

ri ey oo ∞ ff

LINE DESIGN

If the design of the word is determined by the letter spacing, in a sentence the word spacing plays an all-important part: if the spaces are too small, the separate words cannot be distinguished from each other and the sentence becomes practically illegible; if the spaces are too large they detract from the look of the line. The horizontal image – the line – is a guide for the eye. The more cohesion there is in this horizontal line, the more easily it can be read. The letter space should not be bigger than the interior space of the letter 'o'. It may, on the other hand, be so narrow that it is only just possible to see where the new word begins.

TEXT DESIGN

Designing the text means deciding on the width of the margins around the text and the space between individual lines. The margins around the top, the bottom, the fore-edge and along the gutter – the centre fold between two pages in a book – are not wasted paper: they draw attention to the text. If the margins are too narrow, the text seems dispersed over the page and becomes difficult to read. If the margins are too wide, the text disappears. If the piece of work is to be framed, a mount may act as the margins, or reinforce them.

These are a few guidelines to good text design:
  The shorter the text, the closer the lines should be to each other.
  The longer the text, the more space there should be between the lines.

The white spaces between the lines should always be stronger than the white spaces between the words. If the opposite is done and the lines are very loose, 'rivers' appear within a text, forming a kind of vertical interlinear spacing.

THE GOLDEN RULE

For most calligraphers, but particularly for anyone who wants to embark on book work, it is important to know how to design a page. In the thirteenth century Villard de Honnecourt, an architect from Picardy in France, devised an ingenious method of finding the so-called 'golden rule', the optimum proportions for margins, text area and decorations on a book page. This method is applicable to any page size.

Here is how it works:

1) Draw the long diagonals AD, CB.
2) Draw the short diagonals CE, DE.
3) Draw the vertical FG.
4) Draw the line GH.
5) You now have the vital point Q. Draw horizontal lines to cut CB and vertical lines to ED to obtain perfect text margins.

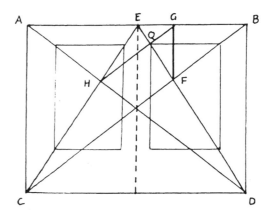

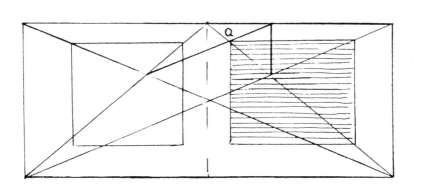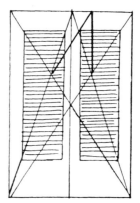

Examples of different book shapes and the text and margin layouts which evolve by using the 'golden rule'.

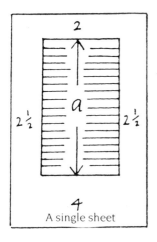

A single sheet

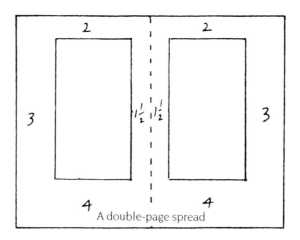

A double-page spread

The last two examples at the bottom of page 65 illustrate the method devised by Edward Johnston to produce well-proportioned pages. As a beginner in calligraphy you may feel that you do not need to know all this, but understanding the underlying principles of the craft from the very beginning will pay dividends when you acquire confidence and want to undertake more ambitious work.

TEXT ARRANGEMENT

As you make progress you will discover for yourself different ways of arranging a block of text. The sketches opposite illustrate some of the possibilities.

a) The bottom margin is always somewhat wider than the top or side margins. As a result of an optical illusion, the text will seem to fit just nicely in the middle of the page.
b) The left and right margins must have about the same 'weight'. To achieve this the left side can also be indented.
c) If the lines are very long (as in a landscape page), then a greater space between the lines is advisable, as this enhances the legibility.
d) If the lines are very short, the space between the lines can be made smaller.

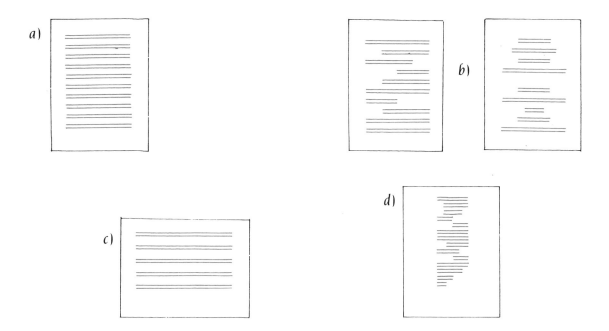

As an exercise, write a few pages of text, using the various permutations illustrated above. To judge them, hang them on the wall and look at them from a distance. You will then see the irregularities clearly: they will show up as dark or light patches in the text. During the planning of a piece of final work you should do several such roughs until you find the arrangement that works best for the piece.

Puer natus est nobis

een Zoon is ons gegeven

ein Kind ist uns geboren

Unto us a Child is born

CAPITALS

As we saw in the introduction to this book, in Carolingian times the practice of using capitals to mark the beginning of a piece of text by writing the first few lines in Roman capitals was already firmly established.

The beginning of a paragraph was marked by uncial letters. A sentence was begun with an oversize minuscule. This is shown in the piece of writing on the right. During the Renaissance the lines already looked as they do today. Ever since, the Roman capital form has been the usual form of capital letter in handwriting as in printing. It is important to understand this form well and appreciate how it fits in the square and the circle. Over the next few pages you will find some exercises which you should practise until you feel confident.

Left. This piece of lettering was prepared for a Christmas card. The large black letters of the Latin inscription make the whole design hang together. The simple decoration reinforces the nativity theme.

INCPNTCAPL
DIALOGE·III·
UBIMULTITUDOHOMI
NUMINSPERATA OCCURRIT
audire g allum defcimar
uniuiratibus locuturo
Ubipuellam duodecennem ab
uteromutam curauit
Ubioleum fuberuf benedicto
necreuit crampulla cumo
leo quod benedixerat fuper

DRAWN CAPITALS

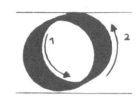

Draw a square to the desired size and divide it into four sections. A circle is drawn inside the square – draw the two diagonals. With this the basic form is ready.

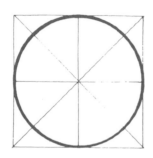

Round letters. We are going to fit the group of 'round letters' into the basic form. The round letters are 'O', 'Q', 'C', 'G' and 'D'. The 'O' has a clear form: the letter fits into the circle.

The 'Q' follows the same pattern, except that at the lower point of intersection of the circle with the diagonal the tail is drawn by following the diagonal.

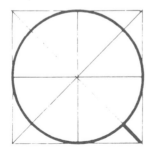
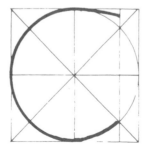

For the 'C', first draw the first half of the circle. The right half is bent slightly outward at the top and bottom and extended to the vertical guideline on the right.

The 'G' is made from the 'C' form. Then the upright line (1–2) is made. In writing with the broad nib a very short horizontal bar towards the inside is added at the top of that upright.

The left upright of the 'D' begins from the top downward. Draw horizontal lines from the top and bottom of the upright line up to the centre of the square, then follow the circle.

Narrowest letters. The 'I' is drawn from top to bottom in one stroke. The 'J' is made in the same way, but the vertical stroke stops at the intersection with the circle and the base of the letter is drawn, following the circle.

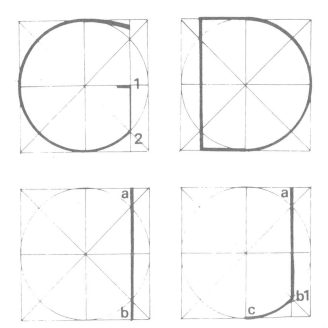

Narrow letters. The letters 'L', 'B', 'P', 'R', 'E', 'F', 'K', and 'S' fit into a half-square. Except for the 'L', these letters consist of a top half and a bottom half. The bottom half is somewhat bigger than the top half. The centre is shifted upwards because of an optical effect. The bottom half of the letter undergoes a similar shift towards the right. These subtle adjustments preserve the form of the square.

71

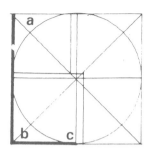

The 'L' consists of a vertical stroke (a–b). The horizontal bar is drawn from b to c.

The 'B'. By enlarging the bottom square as described on the previous page, the upper curve of the 'B' becomes somewhat smaller than the bottom one.

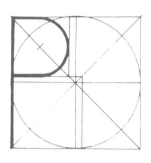
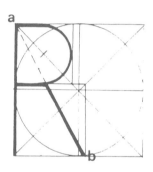

The 'P' is composed of an upright stroke with the upper curve of the 'B' attached to it.

The 'R' is the 'P' with the foot attached as shown, using the line a–b.

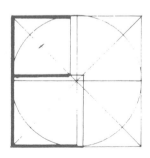
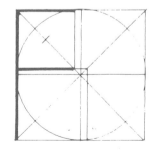

In the 'E' the top two crossbars are equally long, but the bottom one is a little longer to give the letter its equilibrium.

In the 'F' the two crossbars are of the same length.

72

The two diagonal lines of the 'K' form an angle where they meet the perpendicular stroke on the upper line of the lower square.

The 'S' is a difficult letter to draw. Its basic shape fits in the opposite half of the square in which we have drawn the previous letters. To make it easier to achieve, circles have been drawn in the two right-hand squares. The 'S' is slightly bent open at its beginning and its end (like 'C'). You can then follow the circle form.

Wide or rectangular letters. These are 'H', 'A', 'V', 'N', 'U', 'T', 'X' and 'Y'. First draw the two upright lines which will contain the width of these letters.

For the 'H' the two upright strokes are drawn downward and the horizontal bar comes slightly above the centre line for the right optical effect.

For the 'A' draw the two diagonals and add the

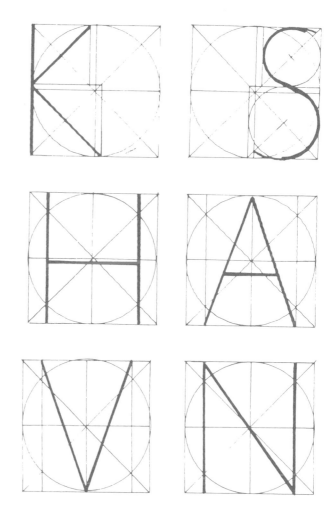

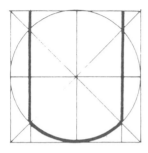
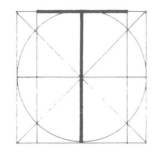
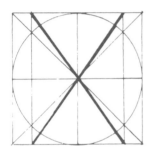
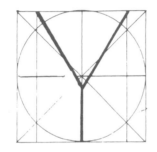
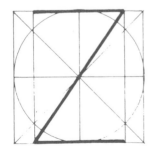

horizontal bar well below the centre to balance the interior white space of the letter.

In the 'V' the two diagonals come together at the centre point at the bottom. It is in fact an upside-down 'A'.

The 'N'. Again draw the vertical strokes first, then the diagonal from the upper left to the lower right.

The base of the 'U' is formed by a section of the circle drawn inside the square. The abrupt transition between the uprights and the arc must be smoothed out.

For the 'T' make the horizontal bar first. The vertical stroke can then be placed precisely in the centre.

The 'X' is formed by the two diagonals. Sometimes the upper starting points are made slightly narrower, and then the centre is placed slightly higher too.

The two diagonals of the 'Y' meet below the centre point; from there the perpendicular line is drawn.

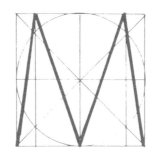

The 'Z' follows the top line to the right, goes diagonally from right to left and follows the baseline to the right.

Very wide letters. The last two letters are the 'M' and the 'W'. Both have the 'V' as a central form, but they are not just upside-down versions of each other.

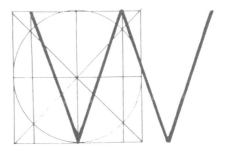

For the 'M', first make the 'V' form in the centre, then draw the two outside strokes. The 'M' fits exactly inside the square.

The 'W' consists of two letters 'V' put side by side. 'W' is the only letter which falls outside the square format. The lines of the 'W' may run parallel, but those of the 'M' never.

When you have practised drawing these letters with the help of the circle in the square, try doing it freehand. It is vital to practise these simple drawn capitals before attempting a more decorative style. Overleaf there is an example of these simplified capitals.

O CGQDH

AVNUTX

YZBEFKL

PRSIJMW

ROMAN CAPITALS

As we said earlier, Roman capitals are at the origin of all capital letters. These, however, were carved out in stone as, for instance, in the magnificent Trajan's column in Rome. The letters shown in the following pages are not true copies of Roman capitals but a simplified version of them. They show all the conventions to do with thickness of strokes, proportions of letters and serifs, but they cannot be produced by simple strokes of the pen – they must be drawn in outline first. The lower-case letters which form part of this alphabet are given on page 79.

A B C D

E F G H I

J K L M
N O P Q
R S T U V
W X Y Z

ROMAN MINUSCULES

These lower-case letters can be used in conjunction with the capitals shown over the previous pages.

a b c d e f

g h i j k l

m n o p q
r s t u v
w x y z

It is good practice to draw each letter in pencil first. It will help to ensure that thick and thin strokes are the correct width throughout the piece if when you start you mark the required thicknesses on a scrap of paper and use this to set out the measurements of each letter. A small set square can be placed on the baseline to ensure that the vertical lines of the letters are straight.

ITALIC STYLE – PEN LETTERING

This style of script (or of type) in which the letters slope slightly to the right evolved in Italy during the Renaissance. Italic developed as a means of writing long documents more quickly than was possible with the more formal scripts. Italic is based on the oval not the circle.

There are, of course, many different styles of italics but on the whole they share the characteristic elongated ascenders and descenders. They also often have flourishes at the extremities. A point to remember is that longer ascenders and descenders will require wider line spacings to allow the eye to travel along the line unimpeded. Flourishes can look wonderful, but they should be used sparingly and appear to grow out of a letter – not grafted on. Successful flourishes require a practised hand and an acute sense of organization if you are doing them freehand, or careful design at the rough stage when you plan a formal piece.

When writing an italic letter the pen is held at a higher angle (about 45 degrees) of thin to horizontal line and the pen stroke is at times pushed upward, something which was advised against in the previous styles studied in this book as creating a tension between the nib and the paper. It is vital to avoid any pressure of pen on writing surface. The thickness of the strokes in proportion to the x-height is also reduced when compared with Roman, as it would interfere with these occasional upward strokes. Overleaf you will find an italic alphabet.

a b c d e f g h

i j k l m n o

p q r s t u v

& w x y z

Y
Z
A B C D E F
G H I J K L
M N O P Q R
S T U V W X &

PREPARING ARTWORK FOR PRINT

On the right-hand page you can see at reduced scale a calligraphic piece which was commissioned for a book jacket. The original artwork was done to about twice the size and reduced to fit the cover. This is good policy as the reduction process tends to 'tighten' the line artwork and make small inaccuracies – inevitable in a piece of calligraphy – less visible.

A transparent overlay is fixed over the top of the prepared black artwork and the printing instructions are marked on it.

Illumination for Modern Calligraphers

PRACTICAL IDEAS FROM NINETEENTH-CENTURY HANDBOOKS

Christopher Jarman

PRINTING IN TWO COLOURS

Camera ready artwork which will be reproduced as line should be made in opaque black ink on plain white paper which can then be mounted on to mounting or ivory board. The piece of work shown on the previous page is printed in two colours. As the colour involves entire groups of words, the artwork can be marked, using a non-repro blue pen or on an overlay, as shown in the sketch on page 84. The size to which the artwork is to be reproduced should be marked, as well as the positioning of the lettering in relation to the shape and size of the cover. It is important that all the instructions are clearly written in ink (a copy should be kept) to avoid unpleasantness and extra costs in case of mistakes. It is always advisable to have written artwork proof-read and approved by the client before passing it on for printing. Line artwork is easy to correct. If a letter has been left out or is not pleasing, it can be remade on a separate scrap of paper and 'cut into' the word.

On the opposite page you will find the same piece of artwork, printed in two colours yet again, but this time the colour separation is a little more complex as single letters appear in black and they will need to be carefully registered with the rest of the words which will appear in red. These initials and the subtitle which are in black should be presented on an overlay (see a) on page 88) while the artwork which will appear in red should be on the main board, see b). Draw accurate corner marks to ensure that everything is in register. If the subtitle, for example, were to print in a third colour, it too should be pasted on a different overlay and the shade clearly specified with a Pantone colour.

Illumination for Modern Calligraphers

PRACTICAL IDEAS FROM NINETEENTH-CENTURY HANDBOOKS

Christopher Jarman

a)

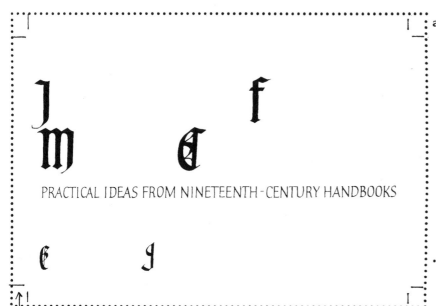

PRACTICAL IDEAS FROM NINETEENTH-CENTURY HANDBOOKS

The artwork has been presented on a board and an overlay. Corner marks are to be accurately placed as they will ensure good register in the finished printed piece.

└ everything on this overlay : solid black

b)

llumination or odern alligraphers

hristopher arman

everything on his overlay : red, Pantone 193 U →

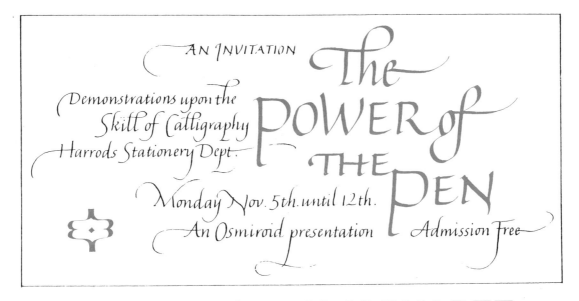

A FORMAL ROMAN ALPHABET

Over the next few pages you will find a set of Roman capitals which are more formal and closer in style to their antique forebears than the alphabet shown on pages 77 to 80. Remember not to exaggerate the gently curving serifs. These should never interfere with the basic shape of the letters.

Using the characteristics of these capitals and adapting the basic shapes of the Roman lower-case letters shown on pages 79-80, you can produce a matching set of minuscules to accompany these capitals.

A B C D
E F G H

I J K L

M N O

P Q R S

T U V

W X Y

Z & !?

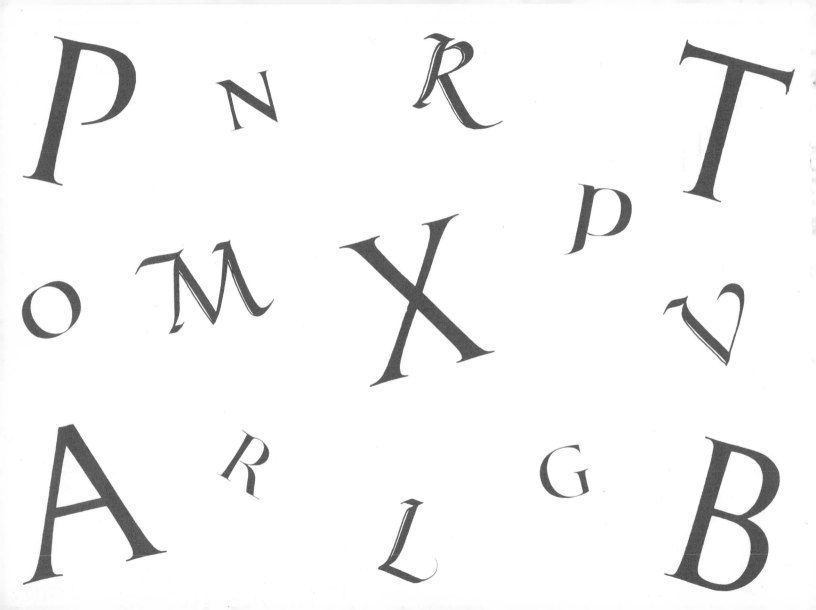